The Circle Of Time

Salwa Rahman

/ BookLeaf
Publishing

India | USA | UK

Made with ❤ on the BookLeaf Publishing Platform

www.bookleafpub.in

www.bookleafpub.com

Dedication

To my past, present, and future

Preface

We are all connected by our thoughts, words, and our actions. However, we never seem to notice that the world around us is what truly brings us together. We cannot know everything, yet we question everything. That is the very essence of our being.

Acknowledgements

To my friends who have always stood by me.
To Azalea, for introducing me to the greatest light there
is.
To my sister, Sabiha, for always supporting me.
To my readers, thank you for stepping into this world
with me.

1. The Past

Though I may feel beautiful,
I know that I can never be like you.
I can never be free.
I can never wear a beautiful dress.
I can never dance on the road.
I can never feel the wind dance with my hair,
entangled with its knots,
and the bruises of my past.
I wish to let it all go, like a feather.
But it is not fair to compare my past to a feather.
My past likes to pick me up,
and cradle me in its arms.
It tells me that it will all be okay,
but how does it know?
It sings me sweet lullabies,
and makes sure to keep me fed.
Eventually,
I would try to let it all go.
I attempt to take my first steps,
but the past does not allow me this freedom.
I would squirm in its grasp,
but it would be too powerful.
Currently,
I can only hold on,

and now my trust is in my past.

2. Belonging

There is so much that I wish to see.
I wish to see all of the stars,
present in the eyes which meet mine.
I wish to watch the birds fly;
to join them as they roam freely.
I want to see those around me,
engulfed by all different kinds of emotions.
I wish to see the joy on one's face,
as they hear the greatest news of their life.
I wish to see the sadness on one's face,
and I wish to embrace them.
I wish to embrace another,
and to share my world with them.
I must remind myself though,
that *this world does not belong to me.*

3. Home

We all begin at once, but how could that be?
We tremble as our fears follow one another.
Each breath we make,
Each step we take,
We are following completely different paths,
Our visions blurry each time we'd look ahead.
Not even the sun could guide us,
Not even the moon.
On our paths,
We think constantly of the places we haven't reached,
We think constantly of the memories we've once lived,
We think constantly of those we've lost.
Even though we're on our own,
We still share the world,
Once we reach the finish line,
But can we ever truly see the finish line?
Or is it just a thought?
It took me time to realize,
There's no true guide.
Nobody else, and nothing else,
Can speak to you as you're on this path.
They can pull you back,
And they can hold you still,
But still you'll continue.

Not for the sake of having an achievement,
Not for the sake of saying you finally made it,
But for the sake of bringing yourself home;
Home, where it all began,
Home, where it all ended.
Perhaps, home isn't a place.
Perhaps, it is a feeling that we must chase,
Maybe it is more than we can imagine.
It hits us at different stages,
Yet affects us all the same.
Maybe there is no real order of things,
And chaos is what keeps us human.
We all begin at once, but how could that be?

4. Time

Some may say that we're running out of time,
but this is not true.
Time is always upon us.
It wakes us,
It carries us,
It pushes us,
And it heals us;
Just as though it were the wind pushing the seas,
Moving them miles from where they once were.
Time does all the same to you and I.
Perhaps it isn't something that is fleeting,
But is what forever lives by us.
It is always there,
Reminding us that it will never leave.
The fears we feel,
The hope we hold,
Time carries it all.
It holds your hand,
A reminder that you are never alone.
The pain you once felt,
Time has faded away.
The fear you once felt,
Time fought it off.
It is always with us,

For as long as we may share the same breath,
Yet some may say that we're running out of time.

5. The World

A cruel world it is,
But she tries to find its beauty.
She tries to find life,
In the dead of the trees.
She tries to see the truth,
In the sea of lies.
She never believes them,
But still, she seeks their truth.
She is chaotic,
A dream,
a mess,
A villain,
And a hero.
She does not know it now,
But when she grows,
She will realize,
That the world has not been as cruel as it once was,
Because she is the beauty she sought for all her life.

6. The Sky

As my gaze focuses on the night's sky,
Watching as it stays still,
The stars, they shine, yet they don't seem to move.
I wonder why that is,
To be such a brave thing which remains so calm.
They omit great brightness,
Yet are nowhere near blinding.
I can see them all so clearly.
It's almost as if I could understand them.
I knew I couldn't,
What a silly thought that must've been.
I couldn't see the clouds,
But I knew they were there.
There is no way they disappear when the sun breaks.
There was more.
The night's sky was more than just the stars.
I saw everything.
I saw the memories I've once cherished,
Intermingling with the ones that I've forgotten.
They battled with the memories I've fought away,
Yet shared the same space.
I found the many pieces of myself,
That I felt I'd never see again.
What a wonderful yet terrifying sight,

To see myself, but to not be able to reach myself.
I can't change the weight of my thoughts which sewed
themselves into the clouds.
I can't stop the starry sky from raining.
I drowned in all its light, in all its glory.
I felt the warmth of its love,
Yet the cold of its unsureness.
I wish I could understand it,
I really do.
It's as if it's both taunting and consoling me,
As if it were my friend and enemy,
As if it were my beginning and ending;
I can't help but keep my gaze rested upon the night's
sky,
Watching as it stays still.

7. You

I thought my feelings worked in a cycle;
that certain feelings would find me,
At certain points in my life.
This is entirely false.
Real emotion is sudden;
Real emotion is raw,
crashing into me when I'd least expect it.
When it hits me,
I truly feel it.
I am so full of emotion,
that it's impossible to feel just one.
I know I have made some mistakes,
And perhaps I never apologized enough.
When I feel this way,
It feels like the world has forgiven me.
I am so full of light.
Light seeping through my heart,
which was once locked away in its cage.
I am so full of you,
Even though I fear to admit it.
I thought my feelings worked in a cycle,
But you changed everything.

8. Wind

I used to think that the future was never written,
and that no decision would affect the next.
What a silly thought it was,
as the wind needs to be pushed by some force;
some force I was never aware of.
Like the wind,
I cannot see what is ahead of me;
I cannot tell where I will find myself.
With each step I take, I feel all the same.
When I look back, everything has completely changed.
Change is not something you notice right away;
it hits you when you least expect it to.
I feel all the same,
yet every part of me has changed.
even when I feel lost,
I am still being pushed forward.

9. The Days

As the world has done its course,
I wonder if I have done any good.
Being productive, active, and kind,
What does it all achieve?
What is love,
if it's always been unknown?
I sit in a pit of despair as I piece myself together,
but these pieces have no home.
I was never one to question,
But there is so much I do not know.
What good is meant for me,
If my heart and mind cannot make amends?
As the days pass,
And the world has done its course,
I wonder if I have done any good.

10. Lost

When you are lost,
the world around you changes.
The air feels heavier,
The days are shorter,
and the nights get colder.
You do not know what's next,
and that terrifies you.
You wish you could turn back time,
but what is there to return to?
Even in the past,
you were lost.
You were always this way;
yet you mourn versions of yourself that you never loved.
You miss what wasn't meant for you,
You miss those who were never there for you.
It's an endless cycle, really,
of missing what you can no longer have.
You are aware that your opportunities are endless,
yet you cannot push yourself to seek them.
You salvage what you have,
when you never had anything to begin with.
The heaviness in the air pushes you back,
the shorter days limit you,
and the colder nights trap you;

The world changes around you,
when you are lost.

11. Love

Your skin holds everything together.
It patches up all of your little mistakes,
And is always forgiving.
Your skin loves you,
And does not care if you do not love it back.
All it asks of you, however,
is to never turn yourself into paper.
Do not let others write on you,
Because they do not write like you.
Your words are poetry,
And your mind is a work of art.
Your sweet smile,
One that cannot be forgotten,
And your sincerest apologies,
That one can only forgive;
Your eyes are my favorite part, my dear,
They continue to sparkle-
Even after you have cried;
even after all that you have lost.
You're nothing close to an angel,
And perfection is but a concept.
but you will always touch my heart,
And I will always love you.

12. Heart

Sometimes,
I feel that my heart is fragile,
but this is far from true.
As soft as it may be,
It has been proven to be the strongest part of me.
Through the blizzards of my sadness,
and the pouring of my solitude,
love has always prevailed.
Through the times it has been shattered,
and the times it has been bruised,
my heart has always mended itself.
Still, I wear it on my sleeve.
It is as though my heart is all over me,
rather just in its cage.
It is a free thing,
one which wants nothing but to grant me safety.
Whether I feel surrounded at loss,
or alone in my triumphs,
my heart continues on.

13. The Trees

Trees remind me of the circle of life.
We get to see them reborn each year;
We see them as their ends meet.
They feather away into the breath of the wind's dancing.
They spin before they fall upon the cold earth;
falling ever so graciously.
As we reach our ends,
We are not aware of what life will bring about.
Perhaps, it won't always be so beautiful.
What we begin with will follow us until the end.
We do not expect it,
and so we fear the ugliness which may rise.
I wish we were like the trees,
but this isn't possible;
We only live once,
and can only rest once.

14. Trapped

Moving freely has always been a task much too difficult.
Flowing with the wind,
And staying afloat upon the raging waters.
Sometimes,
I feel that I have been moving backwards.
Pushing against things that I was meant to pull,
Pulling things I was meant to push.
The shackles which once restrained me,
Have been broken for a while now.
It seems to me now,
that the real trap lies within.

15. Changes

Everything has changed.
Not with you, not with the world,
But with me.
I've created these walls,
Which become see-through with the snap of my fingers;
Which open with the cracks formed by the screaming;
Which becomes a barrier between the tears I let out,
And the world which surrounds me.
Part of me wants to deny it,
The desiccating corpse that I see when I look into the
broken glass;
The pieces of my broken heart, mocking the one beating
inside my chest.
I look at my skin, and I wonder,
Is this all real?
Is this the reality that I've been dealt with?
I pull on it, hoping that it'd easily tear off,
But it does not budge.
In my head though, it has readily detached from my
bones,
But why do I still see it?
Why do I still see the very barrier between what holds
me up?

Why do I feel like I am two entirely different people?

16. Sweetness

There is a lot of sweetness that you cannot taste.
it surrounds you,
being encountered by all that meets your eyes.
Is it really sweet?
You can't taste it,
so you cannot know if it is.
It could be bitter.
It could taste like betrayal.
You would be hurt,
but you do not care.
You have begun to question everything,
while at the same time,
not at all.
You have accepted all that you have lost,
but still, you hope for it all to return.
What you remember,
are not necessarily the good moments.
You remember how you felt,
and often would confuse venom with a cure.
You remember the hurt,
but not how it felt.

17. Shears

We're all complex beings, but I feel out of place;
as if I belong nowhere.
No matter how much I try to hide my wounds,
I fear that others can see them.
They can see the blood seeping through my clothes.
They can see it in my eyes.
They can see it in the way I move,
the way I talk,
the way I am.
It makes me feel vulnerable,
like a sheep stripped of its wool.
In my instance,
I am the one holding the shears;
I was the one most brutal to myself.
I wish I could undo what I have done,
but my dear, I'm afraid it's too late.
As I try to better myself,
I come to realize,
they will never notice this.
They will never try to understand me.
I don't wish to hurt, yet I do so effortlessly.
I hurt more than I love.
Maybe, I hurt due to its *absence*.

18. Staying

We live fast paced lives,
and it is very unsettling.
However,
This is the scariest of them all:
Those who slow down in the midst of the chaos.
You lie within the calm before the storm,
yet you do not realize it.
You feel at ease,
but eventually, you will be caught in the midst of
destruction.
You don't know it yet,
but you're diving into it head-first.
No one can save you.
The only way out of this is through.
Either you make it out with scars and bruises,
or you stay behind for as long as you live.
I chose to stay.

19. Driving

There's too much to carry.
There's the air, the tree, the leaves,
And much more beyond that.
You have to carry yourself no matter the circumstances.
What a grave punishment that must be,
To have to deal with what we've never asked for
To find ourselves holding the handles.
You hold the handles to save yourself,
But you forgot that you're the driver.
By the time you let go of the wheels,
You lost all control.
You spiraled in many directions,
On roads leading further from yourself.
The air heavy and the wind violent,
You can't save yourself.
Eventually, someone else takes over.
They knew they had to lead you home.
You look at them,
Shifting between both of their eyes.
You felt a similar heaviness,
But this time, it was warm.
This time, it was love.
You couldn't look away,

And they won't let go.
They'll take you home.

20. Reflections

As my eyes grazed the sea below,
Her eyes met mine.
I looked into her eyes.
I couldn't talk to her,
I couldn't touch her.
In that moment,
She appeared to be kind, yet volatile,
As the current gently guided the waves.
The sky's sweet freedom stood behind her.
A clear picture which moved restlessly.
I looked forward,
Noticing that the sea's voyage was endless.
What a beautiful feat it must be,
Having to do nothing but to just be;
To move forward, no matter one's defeats.
I looked down and wondered,
Will she too live a life of endless swaying?
What will she carry with her?
I envied her.
Unlike her, I was stuck,
As though I was glued to the rustling earth.
The weight of my past pulls me down.
The weight of my present pushes me back.
The weight of my future keeps me in constraints.

For her, it seemed too easy.

I found no trace of fear in her eyes.

Perhaps life's motions aren't meant to be questioned,

And instead are meant to be experienced.

As the waves continued their venture,

She would too,

even after I would walk away.

She wouldn't know of her destination,

but would only continue her journey;

In all but one direction.

One day,

She will return.

I'll look down once more,

And her eyes will meet mine.

21. The Future

There is no future.
Every day which passes,
Every hour, every minute, every second;
each moment is fleeting.
The fear that we feel,
Isn't just a feeling.
It too becomes a memory.
Memories are beautiful,
And they are always missed,
But they will never return;
they will only linger about our minds.
The reason we continue to live for the future,
Is because we wish to escape the past,
but the past is forever.
As these memories hold us back,
we hold them in return.

www.ingramcontent.com/pod-product-compliance
Lightning Source LLC
Chambersburg PA
CBHW051000030426
42339CB00007B/415